John Greenleaf Whittier

National Lyrics

John Greenleaf Whittier

National Lyrics

ISBN/EAN: 9783744792783

Printed in Europe, USA, Canada, Australia, Japan

Cover: Foto ©Thomas Meinert / pixelio.de

More available books at **www.hansebooks.com**

BY

JOHN GREENLEAF WHITTIER.

.With Illustrations by
GEORGE G. WHITE, H. FENN, AND CHARLES A. BARRY.

BOSTON:
TICKNOR AND FIELDS.
1866.

CONTENTS.

	Page
STANZAS	7
CLERICAL OPPRESSORS	11
THE CHRISTIAN SLAVE	13
STANZAS FOR THE TIMES	15
THE FAREWELL	18
LINES ON READING THE MESSAGE OF GOVERNOR RITNER	21
MASSACHUSETTS TO VIRGINIA	23
THE BRANDED HAND	27
TEXAS	29
TO FANEUIL HALL	33
THE PINE-TREE	34
LINES SUGGESTED BY A VISIT TO WASHINGTON	36
YORKTOWN	40
THE WATCHERS	43
LINES WRITTEN ON THE ADOPTION OF PINCKNEY'S RESOLUTIONS, ETC.	46
THE CRISIS	48
RANDOLPH OF ROANOKE	51
THE ANGELS OF BUENA VISTA	55
DEMOCRACY	58
THY WILL BE DONE	61
"EIN FESTE BURG IST UNSER GOTT"	62
ASTRÆA AT THE CAPITOL	65
THE PASS OF THE SIERRA	67
THE BATTLE AUTUMN OF 1862	69
MITHRIDATES AT CHIOS	71
THE PROCLAMATION	72
AT PORT ROYAL	74
ICHABOD	78
OUR STATE	79

CONTENTS.

STANZAS FOR THE TIMES — 1850	80
A SABBATH SCENE	82
RANTOUL	86
BROWN OF OSSAWATOMIE	89
THE RENDITION	90
LINES ON THE PASSAGE OF THE PERSONAL LIBERTY BILL	91
THE POOR VOTER ON ELECTION DAY	93
THE EVE OF ELECTION	94
LE MARAIS DU CYGNE	97
BARBARA FRIETCHIE	100
LAUS DEO	103

NOT unto us who did but seek
    The word that burned within to speak,
Not unto us this day belong
The triumph and exultant song.

Upon us fell in early youth
The burden of unwelcome truth,
And left us, weak and frail and few,
The censor's painful work to do.

Thenceforth our life a fight became,
The air we breathed was hot with blame;
For not with gauged and softened tone
We made the bondman's cause our own.

We bore, as Freedom's hope forlorn,
The private hate, the public scorn;
Yet held through all the paths we trod
Our faith in man and trust in God.

We prayed and hoped; but still, with awe,
The coming of the sword we saw;
We heard the nearing steps of doom,
And saw the shade of things to come.

In grief which they alone can feel
Who from a mother's wrong appeal,

With blended lines of fear and hope
We cast our country's horoscope.

For still within her house of life
We marked the lurid sign of strife,
And, poisoning and embittering all,
We saw the star of Wormwood fall.

Deep as our love for her, became
Our hate of all that wrought her shame,
And if, thereby, with tongue and pen
We erred, — we were but mortal men.

We hoped for peace: our eyes survey
The blood-red dawn of Freedom's day;
We prayed for love to loose the chain;
'T is shorn by battle's axe in twain!

Not skill nor strength nor zeal of ours
Has mined and heaved the hostile towers;
Not by our hands is turned the key
That sets the sighing captives free.

A redder sea than Egypt's wave
Is piled and parted for the slave;
A darker cloud moves on in light,
A fiercer fire is guide by night!

The praise, O Lord! be Thine alone,
In Thy own way Thy work be done!
Our poor gifts at Thy feet we cast,
To whom be glory, first and last!

3d Mo., 1865.

NATIONAL LYRICS.

STANZAS.

OUR fellow-countrymen in chains!
 Slaves — in a land of light and law!
Slaves — crouching on the very plains
 Where rolled the storm of Freedom's war!

NATIONAL LYRICS.

A groan from Eutaw's haunted wood —
  A wail where Camden's martyrs fell —
By every shrine of patriot blood,
  From Moultrie's wall and Jasper's well!

By storied hill and hallowed grot,
  By mossy wood and marshy glen,
Whence rang of old the rifle-shot,
  And hurrying shout of Marion's men!
The groan of breaking hearts is there —
  The falling lash — the fetter's clank!
Slaves — SLAVES are breathing in that air,
  Which old De Kalb and Sumter drank!

What, ho! — *our* countrymen in chains!
  The whip on WOMAN's shrinking flesh!
Our soil yet reddening with the stains,
  Caught from her scourging, warm and fresh!
What! mothers from their children riven!
  What! God's own image bought and sold!
AMERICANS to market driven,
  And bartered as the brute for gold!

Speak! shall their agony of prayer
  Come thrilling to our hearts in vain?
To us whose fathers scorned to bear
  The paltry *menace* of a chain;
To us, whose boast is loud and long
  Of holy Liberty and Light —
Say, shall these writhing slaves of Wrong,
  Plead vainly for their plundered Right?

What! shall we send, with lavish breath,
  Our sympathies across the wave,
Where Manhood, on the field of death,
  Strikes for his freedom, or a grave?
Shall prayers go up, and hymns be sung
  For Greece, the Moslem fetter spurning,
And millions hail with pen and tongue
  Our light on all her altars burning?

Shall Belgium feel, and gallant France,
   By Vendome's pile and Schoenbrun's wall,
And Poland, gasping on her lance,
   The impulse of our cheering call?
And shall the SLAVE, beneath our eye,
   Clank o'er *our* fields his hateful chain?
And toss his fettered arms on high,
   And groan for Freedom's gift, in vain?

Oh, say, shall Prussia's banner be
   A refuge for the stricken slave?
And shall the Russian serf go free
   By Baikal's lake and Neva's wave?
And shall the wintry-bosomed Dane
   Relax the iron hand of pride,
And bid his bondmen cast the chain
   From fettered soul and limb, aside?

Shall every flap of England's flag
   Proclaim that all around are free,
From "farthest Ind" to each blue crag
   That beetles o'er the Western Sea?
And shall we scoff at Europe's kings,
   When Freedom's fire is dim with us,
And round our country's altar clings
   The damning shade of Slavery's curse?

Go — let us ask of Constantine
   To loose his grasp on Poland's throat;
And beg the lord of Mahmoud's line
   To spare the struggling Suliote —
Will not the scorching answer come
   From turbaned Turk, and scornful Russ:
"Go, loose your fettered slaves at home,
   Then turn, and ask the like of us!"

Just God! and shall we calmly rest,
   The Christian's scorn — the heathen's mirth —
Content to live the lingering jest
   And by-word of a mocking Earth?

Shall our own glorious land retain
  That curse which Europe scorns to bear?
Shall our own brethren drag the chain
  Which not even Russia's menials wear?

Up, then, in Freedom's manly part,
  From gray-beard eld to fiery youth,
And on the nation's naked heart
  Scatter the living coals of Truth!
Up — while ye slumber, deeper yet
  The shadow of our fame is growing!
Up — while ye pause, our sun may set
  In blood, around our altars flowing!

Oh! rouse ye, ere the storm comes forth —
  The gathered wrath of God and man —
Like that which wasted Egypt's earth,
  When hail and fire above it ran.
Hear ye no warnings in the air?
  Feel ye no earthquake underneath?
Up — up — why will ye slumber where
  The sleeper only wakes in death?

Up *now* for Freedom! — not in strife
  Like that your sterner fathers saw —
The awful waste of human life —
  The glory and the guilt of war:
But break the chain — the yoke remove,
  And smite to earth Oppression's rod,
With those mild arms of Truth and Love,
  Made mighty through the living God!

Down let the shrine of Moloch sink,
  And leave no traces where it stood;
Nor longer let its idol drink
  His daily cup of human blood:
But rear another altar there,
  To Truth and Love and Mercy given,
And Freedom's gift, and Freedom's prayer,
  Shall call an answer down from Heaven!

CLERICAL OPPRESSORS.

JUST God! — and these are they
    Who minister at thine altar, God of Right!
Men who their hands with prayer and blessing lay
    On Israel's Ark of light!

What! preach and kidnap men?
    Give thanks — and rob thy own afflicted poor?
Talk of thy glorious liberty, and then
    Bolt hard the captive's door?

What! servants of thy own
Merciful Son, who came to seek and save
The homeless and the outcast, — fettering down
    The tasked and plundered slave!

Pilate and Herod, friends!
Chief priests and rulers, as of old, combine!
Just God and holy! is that church, which lends
    Strength to the spoiler, thine?

Paid hypocrites, who turn
Judgment aside, and rob the Holy Book
Of those high words of truth which search and burn
    In warning and rebuke;

Feed fat, ye locusts, feed!
And, in your tasselled pulpits, thank the Lord
That, from the toiling bondman's utter need,
    Ye pile your own full board.

How long, O Lord! how long
Shall such a priesthood barter truth away,
And, in thy name, for robbery and wrong
    At thy own altars pray?

Is not thy hand stretched forth
Visibly in the heavens, to awe and smite?
Shall not the living God of all the earth,
    And heaven above, do right?

Woe, then, to all who grind
Their brethren of a common Father down!
To all who plunder from the immortal mind
    Its bright and glorious crown!

Woe to the priesthood! woe
To those whose hire is with the price of blood —
Perverting, darkening, changing as they go,
    The searching truths of God!

Their glory and their might
Shall perish; and their very names shall be
Vile before all the people, in the light
    Of a world's liberty.

Oh! speed the moment on
When Wrong shall cease — and Liberty, and Love,
And Truth, and Right, throughout the earth be known
    As in their home above.

THE CHRISTIAN SLAVE.

A CHRISTIAN! going, gone!
Who bids for God's own image? — for his grace
Which that poor victim of the market-place
　　Hath in her suffering won?

My God! can such things be?
Hast Thou not said that whatsoe'er is done
Unto thy weakest and thy humblest one,
　　Is even done to Thee?

In that sad victim, then,
Child of thy pitying love, I see Thee stand —
Once more the jest-word of a mocking band,
　　Bound, sold, and scourged again!

A Christian up for sale!
Wet with her blood your whips — o'ertask her frame,
Make her life loathsome with your wrong and shame,
　　Her patience shall not fail!

A heathen hand might deal
Back on your heads the gathered wrong of years,
But her low, broken prayer and nightly tears,
　　Ye neither heed nor feel.

Con well thy lesson o'er,
Thou *prudent* teacher — tell the toiling slave
No dangerous tale of Him who came to save
　　The outcast and the poor.

But wisely shut the ray
Of God's free Gospel from her simple heart,
And to her darkened mind alone impart
　　One stern command — OBEY!

So shalt thou deftly raise
The market price of human flesh; and while
On thee, their pampered guest, the planters smile,
    Thy church shall praise.

Grave, reverend men shall tell
From Northern pulpits how thy work was blest,
While in that vile South Sodom, first and best,
    Thy poor disciples sell.

Oh, shame! the Moslem thrall,
Who, with his master, to the Prophet kneels,
While turning to the sacred Kebla feels
    His fetters break and fall.

Cheers for the turbaned Bey
Of robber-peopled Tunis! he hath torn
The dark slave-dungeons open, and hath borne
    Their inmates into day:

But our poor slave in vain
Turns to the Christian shrine his aching eyes —
Its rites will only swell his market price,
    And rivet on his chain.

God of all right! how long
Shall priestly robbers at thine altar stand,
Lifting in prayer to Thee, the bloody hand
    And haughty brow of wrong?

Oh, from the fields of cane,
From the low rice-swamp, from the trader's cell —
From the black slave-ship's foul and loathsome hell,
    And coffle's weary chain, —

Hoarse, horrible, and strong,
Rises to Heaven that agonizing cry,
Filling the arches of the hollow sky,
    How LONG, O GOD, HOW LONG?

STANZAS FOR THE TIMES.

IS this the land our fathers loved,
    The freedom which they toiled to win?
Is this the soil whereon they moved?
    Are these the graves they slumber in?
Are *we* the sons by whom are borne
The mantles which the dead have worn?

And shall we crouch above these graves,
    With craven soul and fettered lip?
Yoke in with marked and branded slaves,
    And tremble at the driver's whip?
Bend to the earth our pliant knees,
And speak — but as our masters please?

Shall outraged Nature cease to feel?
    Shall Mercy's tears no longer flow?
Shall ruffian threats of cord and steel —
    The dungeon's gloom — the assassin's blow,
Turn back the spirit roused to save
The Truth, our Country, and the Slave?

Of human skulls that shrine was made,
    Round which the priests of Mexico
Before their loathsome idol prayed, —
    Is Freedom's altar fashioned so?
And must we yield to Freedom's God,
As offering meet, the negro's blood?

Shall tongues be mute, when deeds are wrought
    Which well might shame extremest hell?
Shall freemen lock the indignant thought?
    Shall Pity's bosom cease to swell?
Shall Honor bleed? — Shall Truth succumb?
Shall pen, and press, and soul be dumb?

No — by each spot of haunted ground,
    Where Freedom weeps her children's fall —
By Plymouth's rock, and Bunker's mound —
    By Griswold's stained and shattered wall —
By Warren's ghost — by Langdon's shade —
By all the memories of our dead!

By their enlarging souls, which burst
    The bands and fetters round them set —
By the free Pilgrim spirit nursed
    Within our inmost bosoms, yet —
By all above — around — below —
Be ours the indignant answer — NO!

No — guided by our country's laws,
    For truth, and right, and suffering man,
Be ours to strive in Freedom's cause,
    As Christians *may* — as freemen *can!*
Still pouring on unwilling ears
That truth oppression only fears.

What! shall we guard our neighbor still,
    While woman shrieks beneath his rod,
And while he tramples down at will
    The image of a common God!
Shall watch and ward be round him set,
Of Northern nerve and bayonet?

And shall we know and share with him
    The danger and the growing shame?
And see our Freedom's light grow dim,
    Which should have filled the world with flame?
And, writhing, feel, where'er we turn,
A world's reproach around us burn?

Is 't not enough that this is borne?
    And asks our haughty neighbor more?
Must fetters which his slaves have worn,
    Clank round the Yankee farmer's door?
Must he be told, beside his plough,
What he must speak, and when, and how?

Must he be told his freedom stands
  On Slavery's dark foundations strong —
On breaking hearts and fettered hands,
  On robbery, and crime, and wrong?
That all his fathers taught is vain —
That Freedom's emblem is the chain?

Its life — its soul, from slavery drawn?
  False — foul — profane! Go — teach as well
Of holy Truth from Falsehood born!
  Of Heaven refreshed by airs from Hell!
Of Virtue in the arms of Vice!
Of Demons planting Paradise!

Rail on, then, "brethren of the South" —
  Ye shall not hear the truth the less —
No seal is on the Yankee's mouth,
  No fetter on the Yankee's press!
From our Green Mountains to the Sea,
One voice shall thunder — WE ARE FREE!

THE FAREWELL

OF A VIRGINIA SLAVE MOTHER TO HER DAUGHTERS SOLD INTO SOUTHERN BONDAGE.

GONE, gone — sold and gone,
  To the rice-swamp dank and lone.
Where the slave-whip ceaseless swings,
Where the noisome insect stings,

THE FAREWELL.

Where the fever demon strews
Poison with the falling dews,
Where the sickly sunbeams glare
Through the hot and misty air, —
    Gone, gone — sold and gone,
    To the rice-swamp dank and lone,
    From Virginia's hills and waters, —
    Woe is me, my stolen daughters!

    Gone, gone — sold and gone,
    To the rice-swamp dank and lone.
There no mother's eye is near them,
There no mother's ear can hear them;
Never, when the torturing lash
Seams their back with many a gash,
Shall a mother's kindness bless them,
Or a mother's arms caress them.
    Gone, gone — sold and gone,
    To the rice-swamp dank and lone,
    From Virginia's hills and waters, —
    Woe is me, my stolen daughters!

    Gone, gone — sold and gone,
    To the rice-swamp dank and lone.
Oh, when weary, sad, and slow,
From the fields at night they go,
  aint with toil, and racked with pain,
To their cheerless homes again —
There no brother's voice shall greet them —
There no father's welcome meet them.
    Gone, gone — sold and gone,
    To the rice-swamp dank and lone,
    From Virginia's hills and waters, —
    Woe is me, my stolen daughters!

    Gone, gone — sold and gone,
    To the rice-swamp dank and lone,
From the tree whose shadow lay
On their childhood's place of play —

From the cool spring where they drank —
Rock, and hill, and rivulet bank —
From the solemn house of prayer,
And the holy counsels there, —
    Gone, gone — sold and gone,
    To the rice-swamp dank and lone,
    From Virginia's hills and waters, —
    Woe is me, my stolen daughters!

    Gone, gone — sold and gone,
    To the rice-swamp dank and lone.
Toiling through the weary day,
And at night the spoiler's prey.
Oh, that they had earlier died,
Sleeping calmly, side by side,
Where the tyrant's power is o'er,
And the fetter galls no more!
    Gone, gone — sold and gone,
    To the rice-swamp dank and lone,
    From Virginia's hills and waters, —
    Woe is me, my stolen daughters!

    Gone, gone — sold and gone,
    To the rice-swamp dank and lone.
By the holy love He beareth —
By the bruised reed He spareth —
Oh, may He, to whom alone
All their cruel wrongs are known,
Still their hope and refuge prove,
With a more than mother's love.
    Gone, gone — sold and gone,
    To the rice-swamp dank and lone,
    From Virginia's hills and waters, —
    Woe is me, my stolen daughters!

LINES,

WRITTEN ON READING THE MESSAGE OF GOVERNOR RITNER, OF PENNSYLVANIA, 1836.

THANK God for the token! — one lip is still free —
One spirit untrammelled — unbending one knee!
Like the oak of the mountain, deep-rooted and firm,
Erect, when the multitude bends to the storm;
When traitors to Freedom, and Honor, and God,
Are bowed at an Idol polluted with blood;
When the recreant North has forgotten her trust,
And the lip of her honor is low in the dust, —
Thank God, that one arm from the shackle has broken!
Thank God, that one man, as a *freeman* has spoken!

O'er thy crags, Alleghany, a blast has been blown!
Down thy tide, Susquehanna, the murmur has gone!
To the land of the South — of the charter and chain —
Of Liberty sweetened with Slavery's pain;
Where the cant of Democracy dwells on the lips
Of the forgers of fetters, and wielders of whips!
Where "chivalric" honor means really no more
Than scourging of women, and robbing the poor!
Where the Moloch of Slavery sitteth on high,
And the words which he utters are — WORSHIP, OR DIE!

Right onward, oh, speed it! Wherever the blood
Of the wronged and the guiltless is crying to God;
Wherever a slave in his fetters is pining;
Wherever the lash of the driver is twining;
Wherever from kindred, torn rudely apart,
Comes the sorrowful wail of the broken of heart;
Wherever the shackles of tyranny bind,
In silence and darkness, the God-given mind;
There, God speed it onward! — its truth will be felt —
The bonds shall be loosened — the iron shall melt!

And oh, will the land where the free soul of PENN
Still lingers and breathes over mountain and glen —
Will the land where a BENEZET's spirit went forth
To the peeled, and the meted, and outcast of Earth —
Where the words of the Charter of Liberty first
From the soul of the sage and the patriot burst —
Where first for the wronged and the weak of their kind,
The Christian and statesman their efforts combined —
Will that land of the free and the good wear a chain?
Will the call to the rescue of Freedom be vain?

No, RITNER! — her "Friends," at thy warning shall stand
Erect for the truth, like their ancestral band;
Forgetting the feuds and the strife of past time,
Counting coldness injustice, and silence a crime;
Turning back from the cavil of creeds, to unite
Once again for the poor in defence of the Right;
Breasting calmly, but firmly, the full tide of Wrong,
Overwhelmed, but not borne on its surges along;
Unappalled by the danger, the shame and the pain,
And counting each trial for Truth as their gain!

And that bold-hearted yeomanry, honest and true,
Who, haters of fraud, give to labor its due;
Whose fathers, of old, sang in concert with thine,
On the banks of Swetara, the songs of the Rhine —
The German-born pilgrims, who first dared to brave
The scorn of the proud in the cause of the slave: —
Will the sons of such men yield the lords of the South
One brow for the brand — for the padlock one mouth?
They cater to tyrants? — They rivet the chain,
Which their fathers smote off, on the negro again?

No, never! — one voice, like the sound in the cloud,
When the roar of the storm waxes loud and more loud,
Wherever the foot of the freeman hath pressed
From the Delaware's marge to the Lake of the West,
On the South-going breezes shall deepen and grow
Till the land it sweeps over shall tremble below!

The voice of a PEOPLE — uprisen — awake —
Pennsylvania's watchword, with Freedom at stake,
Thrilling up from each valley, flung down from each height,
"OUR COUNTRY AND LIBERTY! — GOD FOR THE RIGHT!"

MASSACHUSETTS TO VIRGINIA.

THE blast from Freedom's Northern hills, upon its Southern way,
Bears greeting to Virginia from Massachusetts Bay : —
No word of haughty challenging, nor battle bugle's peal,
Nor steady tread of marching files, nor clang of horsemen's steel.

No trains of deep-mouthed cannon along our highways go —
Around our silent arsenals untrodden lies the snow ;
And to the land-breeze of our ports, upon their errands far,
A thousand sails of commerce swell, but none are spread for war.

We hear thy threats, Virginia! thy stormy words and high,
Swell harshly on the Southern winds which melt along our sky ;
Yet, not one brown, hard hand foregoes its honest labor here —
No hewer of our mountain oaks suspends his axe in fear.

Wild are the waves which lash the reefs along St. George's bank —
Cold on the shore of Labrador the fog lies white and dank ;
Through storm and wave, and blinding mist, stout are the hearts which man
The fishing-smacks of Marblehead, the sea-boats of Cape Ann.

The cold north light and wintry sun glare on their icy forms,
Bent grimly o'er their straining lines or wrestling with the storms ;
Free as the winds they drive before, rough as the waves they roam,
They laugh to scorn the slaver's threat against their rocky home.

What means the Old Dominion? Hath she forgot the day
When o'er her conquered valleys swept the Briton's steel array?
How side by side, with sons of hers, the Massachusetts men
Encountered Tarleton's charge of fire, and stout Cornwallis, then?

Forgets she how the Bay State, in answer to the call
Of her old House of Burgesses, spoke out from Faneuil Hall?
When, echoing back her Henry's cry, came pulsing on each breath
Of Northern winds, the thrilling sounds of "LIBERTY OR DEATH!"

What asks the Old Dominion? If now her sons have proved
False to their fathers' memory — false to the faith they loved,
If she can scoff at Freedom, and its great charter spurn,
Must we of Massachusetts from truth and duty turn?

We hunt your bondmen, flying from Slavery's hateful hell —
Our voices, at your bidding, take up the bloodhound's yell —
We gather, at your summons, above our fathers' graves,
From Freedom's holy altar-horns to tear your wretched slaves!

Thank God! not yet so vilely can Massachusetts bow;
The spirit of her early time is with her even now;
Dream not because her Pilgrim blood moves slow, and calm, and
    cool,
She thus can stoop her chainless neck, a sister's slave and tool!

All that a *sister* State should do, all that a *free* State may,
Heart, hand, and purse we proffer, as in our early day;
But that one dark loathsome burden ye must stagger with alone,
And reap the bitter harvest which ye yourselves have sown!

Hold, while ye may, your struggling slaves, and burden God's
    free air
With woman's shriek beneath the lash, and manhood's wild de-
    spair;
Cling closer to the "cleaving curse" that writes upon your plains
The blasting of Almighty wrath against a land of chains.

Still shame your gallant ancestry, the cavaliers of old,
By watching round the shambles where human flesh is sold —
Gloat o'er the new-born child, and count his market value, when
The maddened mother's cry of woe shall pierce the slaver's den!

Lower than plummet soundeth, sink the Virginian name;
Plant, if ye will, your fathers' graves with rankest weeds of shame;
Be, if ye will, the scandal of God's fair universe —
We wash our hands forever, of your sin, and shame, and curse.

A voice from lips whereon the coal from Freedom's shrine hath been,
Thrilled, as but yesterday, the hearts of Berkshire's mountain men:
The echoes of that solemn voice are sadly lingering still
In all our sunny valleys, on every wind-swept hill.

And when the prowling man-thief came hunting for his prey
Beneath the very shadow of Bunker's shaft of gray,
How, through the free lips of the son, the father's warning spoke;
How, from its bonds of trade and sect, the Pilgrim city broke!

A hundred thousand right arms were lifted up on high, —
A hundred thousand voices sent back their loud reply;
Through the thronged towns of Essex the startling summons rang,
And up from bench and loom and wheel her young mechanics sprang!

The voice of free, broad Middlesex — of thousands as of one —
The shaft of Bunker calling to that of Lexington —
From Norfolk's ancient villages; from Plymouth's rocky bound
To where Nantucket feels the arms of ocean close her round; —

From rich and rural Worcester, where through the calm repose
Of cultured vales and fringing woods the gentle Nashua flows,
To where Wachuset's wintry blasts the mountain larches stir,
Swelled up to Heaven the thrilling cry of "God save Latimer!"

And sandy Barnstable rose up, wet with the salt sea spray —
And Bristol sent her answering shout down Narragansett Bay !
Along the broad Connecticut old Hampden felt the thrill,
And the cheer of Hampshire's woodmen swept down from Holyoke Hill.

The voice of Massachusetts ! Of her free sons and daughters —
Deep calling unto deep aloud — the sound of many waters !
Against the burden of that voice what tyrant power shall stand ?
No fetters in the Bay State! No slave upon her land!

Look to it well, Virginians ! In calmness we have borne,
In answer to our faith and trust, your insult and your scorn ;
You've spurned our kindest counsels — you've hunted for our lives —
And shaken round our hearths and homes your manacles and gyves !

We wage no war — we lift no arm — we fling no torch within
The fire-damps of the quaking mine beneath your soil of sin ;
We leave ye with your bondmen, to wrestle, while ye can,
With the strong upward tendencies and God-like soul of man !

But for us and for our children, the vow which we have given
For freedom and humanity, is registered in Heaven ;
No slave-hunt in our borders — no pirate on our strand !
No fetters in the Bay State — no slave upon our land !

THE BRANDED HAND.

1846.

WELCOME home again, brave seaman! with thy thoughtful brow and gray,
And the old heroic spirit of our earlier, better day, —
With that front of calm endurance, on whose steady nerve, in vain
Pressed the iron of the prison, smote the fiery shafts of pain!

Is the tyrant's brand upon thee? Did the brutal cravens aim
To make God's truth thy falsehood, his holiest work thy shame?
When, all blood-quenched, from the torture the iron was withdrawn,
How laughed their evil angel the baffled fools to scorn!

They change to wrong, the duty which God hath written out
On the great heart of humanity too legible for doubt!
They, the loathsome moral lepers, blotched from footsole up to crown,
Give to shame what God hath given unto honor and renown!

Why, that brand is highest honor! — than its traces never yet
Upon old armorial hatchments was a prouder blazon set;
And thy unborn generations, as they tread our rocky strand,
Shall tell with pride the story of their father's BRANDED HAND!

As the Templar home was welcome, bearing back from Syrian wars
The scars of Arab lances, and of Paynim scimetars,
The pallor of the prison and the shackle's crimson span,
So we meet thee, so we greet thee, truest friend of God and man!

He suffered for the ransom of the dear Redeemer's grave,
Thou for his living presence in the bound and bleeding slave;
He for a soil no longer by the feet of angels trod,
Thou for the true Shechinah, the present home of God!

For, while the jurist sitting with the slave-whip o'er him swung,
From the tortured truths of freedom the lie of slavery wrung,
And the solemn priest to Moloch, on each God-deserted shrine,
Broke the bondman's heart for bread, poured the bondman's blood
    for wine, —

While the multitude in blindness to a far-off Saviour knelt,
And spurned, the while, the temple where a present Saviour dwelt;
Thou beheld'st Him in the task-field, in the prison-shadows dim,
And thy mercy to the bondman, it was mercy unto Him!

In thy lone and long night-watches, sky above and wave below,
Thou did'st learn a higher wisdom than the babbling schoolmen
    know;
God's stars and silence taught thee, as his angels only can,
That the one, sole sacred thing beneath the cope of heaven, is Man!

That he who treads profanely on the scrolls of law and creed,
In the depth of God's great goodness may find mercy in his need;
But woe to him who crushes the SOUL with chain and rod,
And herds with lower natures the awful form of God!

Then lift that manly right hand, bold ploughman of the wave!
Its branded palm shall prophesy, "SALVATION TO THE SLAVE!"
Hold up its fire-wrought language, that whoso reads may feel
His heart swell strong within him, his sinews change to steel.

Hold it up before our sunshine, up against our Northern air, —
Ho! men of Massachusetts, for the love of God look there!
Take it henceforth for your standard, — like the Bruce's heart of
    yore,
In the dark strife closing round ye, let that hand be seen before!

And the tyrants of the slave-land shall tremble at that sign,
When it points its finger Southward along the Puritan line:
Woe to the State-gorged leeches, and the Church's locust band,
When they look from slavery's ramparts on the coming of that
    hand!

TEXAS.

VOICE OF NEW ENGLAND.

UP the hill-side, down the glen,
   Rouse the sleeping citizen;
Summon out the might of men!

Like a lion growling low —
Like a night-storm rising slow —
Like the tread of unseen foe —

It is coming — it is nigh!
Stand your homes and altars by;
On your own free thresholds die.

Clang the bells in all your spires;
On the gray hills of your sires
Fling to heaven your signal-fires.

From Wachuset, lone and bleak,
Unto Berkshire's tallest peak,
Let the flame-tongued heralds speak.

O, for God and duty stand,
Heart to heart and hand to hand,
Round the old graves of the land.

Whoso shrinks or falters now,
Whoso to the yoke would bow,
Brand the craven on his brow!

Freedom's soil hath only place
For a free and fearless race —
None for traitors false and base.

Perish party — perish clan;
Strike together while ye can,
Like the arm of one strong man.

Like that angel's voice sublime,
Heard above a world of crime,
Crying of the end of time —

With one heart and with one mouth,
Let the North unto the South
Speak the word befitting both:

TEXAS.

" What though Issachar be strong !
Ye may load his back with wrong
Overmuch and over long :

Patience with her cup o'errun,
With her weary thread outspun,
Murmurs that her work is done.

Make our Union-bond a chain,
Weak as tow in Freedom's strain
Link by link shall snap in twain.

Vainly shall your sand-wrought rope
Bind the starry cluster up,
Shattered over heaven's blue cope !

Give us bright though broken rays,
Rather than eternal haze,
Clouding o'er the full-orbed blaze.

Take your land of sun and bloom ;
Only leave to Freedom room
For her plough, and forge, and loom ;

Take your slavery-blackened vales ;
Leave us but our own free gales,
Blowing on our thousand sails.

Boldly, or with treacherous art,
Strike the blood-wrought chain apart ;
Break the Union's mighty heart ;

Work the ruin, if ye will ;
Pluck upon your heads an ill
Which shall grow and deepen still.

With your bondman's right arm bare,
With his heart of black despair,
Stand alone, if stand ye dare !

Onward with your fell design;
Dig the gulf and draw the line:
Fire beneath your feet the mine:

Deeply, when the wide abyss
Yawns between your land and this,
Shall ye feel your helplessness.

By the hearth, and in the bed,
Shaken by a look or tread,
Ye shall own a guilty dread.

And the curse of unpaid toil,
Downward through your generous soil
Like a fire shall burn and spoil.

Our bleak hills shall bud and blow,
Vines our rocks shall overgrow,
Plenty in our valleys flow; —

And when vengeance clouds your skies,
Hither shall ye turn your eyes,
As the lost on Paradise!

We but ask our rocky strand,
Freedom's true and brother band,
Freedom's strong and honest hand, —

Valleys by the slave untrod,
And the Pilgrim's mountain sod,
Blessed of our fathers' God!"

TO FANEUIL HALL.

1844.

MEN! — if manhood still ye claim,
    If the Northern pulse can thrill,
Roused by wrong or stung by shame,
    Freely, strongly still : —
Let the sounds of traffic die :
    Shut the mill-gate — leave the stall —
Fling the axe and hammer by —
    Throng to Faneuil Hall !

Wrongs which freemen never brooked —
    Dangers grim and fierce as they,
Which, like couching lions, looked
    On your father's way ; —
These your instant zeal demand,
    Shaking with their earthquake-call
Every rood of Pilgrim land —
    Ho, to Faneuil Hall !

From your capes and sandy bars —
    From your mountain-ridges cold,
Through whose pines the westering stars
    Stoop their crowns of gold —
Come, and with your footsteps wake
    Echoes from that holy wall :
Once again, for Freedom's sake,
    Rock your fathers' hall !

Up, and tread beneath your feet
    Every cord by party spun ;
Let your hearts together beat
    As the heart of one.

Banks and tariffs, stocks and trade,
  Let them rise or let them fall:
Freedom asks your common aid —
  Up, to Faneuil Hall!

Up, and let each voice that speaks
  Ring from thence to Southern plains,
Sharply as the blow which breaks
  Prison-bolts and chains!
Speak as well becomes the free —
  Dreaded more than steel or ball,
Shall your calmest utterance be,
  Heard from Faneuil Hall!

Have they wronged us? Let us then
  Render back nor threats nor prayers;
Have they chained our free-born men?
  LET US UNCHAIN THEIRS!
Up! your banner leads the van,
  Blazoned "Liberty for all!"
Finish what your sires began —
  Up, to Faneuil Hall!

THE PINE-TREE.

1846.

LIFT again the stately emblem on the Bay State's rusted shield,
Give to Northern winds the Pine-Tree on our banner's tattered field,
Sons of men who sat in council with their Bibles round the board,
Answering England's royal missive with a firm, "THUS SAITH THE LORD!"
Rise again for home and freedom! — set the battle in array! —
What the fathers did of old time we their sons must do to-day.

Tell us not of banks and tariffs — cease your paltry peddler cries —
Shall the good State sink her honor that your gambling stocks
 may rise?
Would ye barter man for cotton? — That your gains may sum
 up higher,
Must we kiss the feet of Moloch, pass our children through the
 fire?
Is the dollar only real? — God and truth and right a dream?
Weighed against your lying ledgers must our manhood kick the
 beam?

O my God! — for that free spirit, which of old in Boston town
Smote the Province House with terror, struck the crest of Andros
 down! —
For another strong-voiced Adams in the city's streets to cry:
" Up for God and Massachusetts! — Set your feet on Mammon's
 lie!
Perish banks and perish traffic — spin your cotton's latest pound —
But in Heaven's name keep your honor — keep the heart o' the
 Bay State sound!"

Where's the MAN for Massachusetts? — Where's the voice to
 speak her free? —
Where's the hand to light up bonfires from her mountains to the
 sea?
Beats her Pilgrim pulse no longer? — Sits she dumb in her de-
 spair? —
Has she none to break the silence? — Has she none to do and
 dare?
O my God! for one right worthy to lift up her rusted shield,
And to plant again the Pine-Tree in her banner's tattered field!

LINES,

SUGGESTED BY A VISIT TO THE CITY OF WASHINGTON IN THE 12TH MONTH OF 1845.

WITH a cold and wintry noon-light,
    On its roofs and steeples shed,
Shadows weaving with the sunlight
    From the gray sky overhead,
Broadly, vaguely, all around me, lies the half-built town outspread.

Through this broad street, restless ever,
    Ebbs and flows a human tide,
Wave on wave a living river;
    Wealth and fashion side by side;
Toiler, idler, slave and master, in the same quick current glide.

Underneath yon dome, whose coping
    Springs above them, vast and tall,
Grave men in the dust are groping
    For the largess, base and small,
Which the hand of Power is scattering, crumbs which from its table fall.

Base of heart! They vilely barter
    Honor's wealth for party's place:
Step by step on Freedom's charter
    Leaving footprints of disgrace;
For to-day's poor pittance turning from the great hope of their race.

Yet, where festal lamps are throwing
    Glory round the dancer's hair,
Gold-tressed, like an angel's flowing
    Backward on the sunset air;
And the low quick pulse of music beats its measures sweet and rare:

There to-night shall woman's glances,
    Star-like, welcome give to them,
Fawning fools with shy advances
    Seek to touch their garments' hem,
With the tongue of flattery glozing deeds which God and Truth
    condemn.

From this glittering lie my vision
    Takes a broader, sadder range,
Full before me have arisen
    Other pictures dark and strange;
From the parlor to the prison must the scene and witness
    change.

Hark! the heavy gate is swinging
    On its hinges, harsh and slow;
One pale prison lamp is flinging
    On a fearful group below
Such a light as leaves to terror whatsoe'er it does not show.

Pitying God! — Is that a WOMAN
    On whose wrist the shackles clash?
Is that shriek she utters human,
    Underneath the stinging lash?
Are they MEN whose eyes of madness from that sad procession
    flash?

Still the dance goes gayly onward!
    What is it to Wealth and Pride?
That without the stars are looking
    On a scene which earth should hide?
That the SLAVE-SHIP lies in waiting, rocking on Potomac's tide!

Vainly to that mean Ambition
    Which, upon a rival's fall,
Winds above its old condition,
    With a reptile's slimy crawl,
Shall the pleading voice of sorrow, shall the slave in anguish
    call?

Vainly to the child of Fashion,
   Giving to ideal woe
Graceful luxury of compassion,
   Shall the stricken mourner go;
Hateful seems the earnest sorrow, beautiful the hollow show!

Nay, my words are all too sweeping;
   In this crowded human mart,
Feeling is not dead, but sleeping;
   Man's strong will and woman's heart,
In the coming strife for Freedom, yet shall bear their generous part.

And from yonder sunny valleys,
   Southward in the distance lost,
Freedom yet shall summon allies
   Worthier than the North can boast,
With the Evil by their hearth-stones grappling at severer cost.

Now, the soul alone is willing.
   Faint the heart and weak the knee;
And as yet no lip is thrilling
   With the mighty words "BE FREE!"
Tarrieth long the land's Good Angel, but his advent is to be!

Meanwhile, turning from the reve'
   To the prison-cell my sight,
For intenser hate of evil,
   For a keener sense of right,
Shaking off thy dust, I thank thee, City of the Slaves, to-night!

"To thy duty now and ever!
   Dream no more of rest or stay;
Give to Freedom's great endeavor
   All thou art and hast to-day":—
Thus, above the city's murmur, saith a Voice, or seems to say.

Ye with heart and vision gifted
   To discern and love the right,

Whose worn faces have been lifted
    To the slowly-growing light,
Where from Freedom's sunrise drifted slowly back the murk of
    night! —

Ye who through long years of trial
    Still have held your purpose fast,
While a lengthening shade the dial
    From the westering sunshine cast,
And of hope each hour's denial seemed an echo of the last! —

O my brothers! O my sisters!
    Would to God that ye were near,
Gazing with me down the vistas
    Of a sorrow strange and drear;
Would to God that ye were listeners to the Voice I seem to hear!

With the storm above us driving,
    With the false earth mined below —
Who shall marvel if thus striving
    We have counted friend as foe;
Unto one another giving in the darkness blow for blow.

Well it may be that our natures
    Have grown sterner and more hard,
And the freshness of their features
    Somewhat harsh and battle-scarred,
And their harmonies of feeling overtasked and rudely jarred.

Be it so. It should not swerve us
    From a purpose true and brave;
Dearer Freedom's rugged service
    Than the pastime of the slave;
Better is the storm above it than the quiet of the grave.

Let us then, uniting, bury
    All our idle feuds in dust,
And to future conflicts carry
    Mutual faith and common trust;
Always he who most forgiveth in his brother is most just.

From the eternal shadow rounding
    All our sun and starlight here,
Voices of our lost ones sounding
    Bid us be of heart and cheer,
Through the silence, down the spaces, falling on the inward ear.

Know we not our dead are looking
    Downward with a sad surprise,
All our strife of words rebuking
    With their mild and loving eyes?
Shall we grieve the holy angels? Shall we cloud their blessed skies?

Let us draw their mantles o'er us
    Which have fallen in our way;
Let us do the work before us,
    Cheerly, bravely, while we may,
Ere the long night-silence cometh, and with us it is not day!

YORKTOWN.

FROM Yorktown's ruins, ranked and still,
    Two lines stretch far o'er vale and hill:
Who curbs his steed at head of one?
Hark! the low murmur: Washington!
Who bends his keen, approving glance
Where down the gorgeous line of France
Shine knightly star and plume of snow?
Thou too art victor, Rochambeau!

The earth which bears this calm array
Shook with the war-charge yesterday,
Ploughed deep with hurrying hoof and wheel,
Shot-sown and bladed thick with steel;

YORKTOWN.

October's clear and noonday sun
Paled in the breath-smoke of the gun,
And down night's double blackness fell,
Like a dropped star, the blazing shell.

Now all is hushed: the gleaming lines
Stand moveless as the neighboring pines;
While through them, sullen, grim, and slow,
The conquered hosts of England go:
O'Hara's brow belies his dress,
Gay Tarleton's troop rides bannerless:
Shout, from thy fired and wasted homes,
Thy scourge, Virginia, captive comes!

Nor thou alone: with one glad voice
Let all thy sister States rejoice;
Let Freedom, in whatever clime
She waits with sleepless eye her time,
Shouting from cave and mountain wood,
Make glad her desert solitude,
While they who hunt her quail with fear:
The New World's chain lies broken here!

But who are they, who, cowering, wait
Within the shattered fortress gate?
Dark tillers of Virginia's soil,
Classed with the battle's common spoil,
With household stuffs, and fowl, and swine,
With Indian weed and planters' wine,
With stolen beeves, and foraged corn, —
Are they not men, Virginian born?

O, veil your faces, young and brave!
Sleep, Scammel, in thy soldier grave!
Sons of the Northland, ye who set
Stout hearts against the bayonet,
And pressed with steady footfall near
The moated battery's blazing tier,
Turn your scarred faces from the sight,
Let shame do homage to the right!

Lo! threescore years have passed; and where
The Gallic timbrel stirred the air,
With Northern drum-roll, and the clear,
Wild horn-blow of the mountaineer,
While Britain grounded on that plain
The arms she might not lift again,
As abject as in that old day
The slave still toils his life away.

O, fields still green and fresh in story,
Old days of pride, old names of glory,
Old marvels of the tongue and pen,
Old thoughts which stirred the hearts of men,
Ye spared the wrong; and over all
Behold the avenging shadow fall!
Your world-wide honor stained with shame, —
Your freedom's self a hollow name!

Where 's now the flag of that old war?
Where flows its stripe? Where burns its star?
Bear witness, Palo Alto's day,
Dark Vale of Palms, red Monterey,
Where Mexic Freedom, young and weak,
Fleshes the Northern eagle's beak:
Symbol of terror and despair,
Of chains and slaves, go seek it there!

Laugh, Prussia, midst thy iron ranks!
Laugh, Russia, from thy Neva's banks!
Brave sport to see the fledgling born
Of Freedom by its parent torn!
Safe now is Speilberg's dungeon cell,
Safe drear Siberia's frozen hell:
With Slavery's flag o'er both unrolled,
What of the New World fears the Old?

THE WATCHERS.

BESIDE a stricken field I stood;
  On the torn turf, on grass and wood,
Hung heavily the dew of blood.

Still in their fresh mounds lay the slain,
But all the air was quick with pain
And gusty sighs and tearful rain.

Two angels, each with drooping head
And folded wings and noiseless tread,
Watched by that valley of the dead.

The one, with forehead saintly bland
And lips of blessing, not command,
Leaned, weeping, on her olive wand.

The other's brows were scarred and knit,
His restless eyes were watch-fires lit,
His hands for battle-gauntlets fit.

"How long!" — I knew the voice of Peace, —
"Is there no respite? — no release?
When shall the hopeless quarrel cease?

"O Lord, how long! — One human soul
Is more than any parchment scroll,
Or any flag thy winds unroll.

"What price was Ellsworth's, young and brave?
How weigh the gift that Lyon gave,
Or count the cost of Winthrop's grave?

"O brother! if thine eye can see,
Tell how and when the end shall be,
What hope remains for thee and me."

Then Freedom sternly said : "I shun
No strife nor pang beneath the sun,
When human rights are staked and won.

"I knelt with Ziska's hunted flock,
I watched in Toussaint's cell of rock,
I walked with Sidney to the block.

"The moor of Marston felt my tread,
Through Jersey snows the march I led,
My voice Magenta's charges sped.

"But now, through weary day and night,
I watch a vague and aimless fight
For leave to strike one blow aright.

"On either side my foe they own:
One guards through love his ghastly throne,
And one through fear to reverence grown.

"Why wait we longer, mocked, betrayed,
By open foes, or those afraid
To speed thy coming through my aid?

"Why watch to see who win or fall? —
I shake the dust against them all,
I leave them to their senseless brawl."

"Nay," Peace implored: "yet longer wait;
The doom is near, the stake is great:
God knoweth if it be too late.

"Still wait and watch; the way prepare
Where I with folded wings of prayer
May follow, weaponless and bare."

"Too late!" the stern, sad voice replied,
"Too late!" its mournful echo sighed,
In low lament the answer died.

A rustling as of wings in flight,
An upward gleam of lessening white,
So passed the vision, sound and sight.

But round me, like a silver bell
Rung down the listening sky to tell
Of holy help, a sweet voice fell.

"Still hope and trust," it sang; "the rod
Must fall, the wine-press must be trod,
But all is possible with God!"

LINES,

WRITTEN ON THE ADOPTION OF PINCKNEY'S RESOLUTIONS, IN THE HOUSE OF REPRESENTATIVES, AND THE PASSAGE OF CALHOUN'S "BILL FOR EXCLUDING PAPERS, WRITTEN OR PRINTED, TOUCHING THE SUBJECT OF SLAVERY FROM THE U. S. POST-OFFICE," IN THE SENATE OF THE UNITED STATES.

MEN of the North-land! where 's the manly spirit
    Of the true-hearted and the unshackled gone?
Sons of old freemen, do we but inherit
          Their names alone?

Is the old Pilgrim spirit quenched within us,
    Stoops the strong manhood of our souls so low,
That Mammon's lure or Party's wile can win us
          To silence now!

Now, when our land to ruin's brink is verging,
    In God's name, let us speak while there is time!
Now, when the padlocks for our lips are forging,
          Silence is crime!

What! shall we henceforth humbly ask as favors
    Rights all our own? In madness shall we barter,
For treacherous peace, the freedom Nature gave us,
          God and our charter?

Here shall the statesman forge his human fetters,
    Here the false jurist human rights deny,
And, in the church, their proud and skilled abettors
          Make truth a lie?

Torture the pages of the hallowed Bible,
    To sanction crime, and robbery, and blood?
And, in Oppression's hateful service, libel
          Both man and God?

LINES.

Shall our New England stand erect no longer,
   But stoop in chains upon her downward way,
Thicker to gather on her limbs and stronger
             Day after day?

O no; methinks from all her wild, green mountains —
   From valleys where her slumbering fathers lie —
From her blue rivers and her welling fountains,
             And clear, cold sky —

From her rough coast, and isles, which hungry Ocean
   Gnaws with his surges — from the fisher's skiff,
With white sail swaying to the billows' motion
             Round rock and cliff —

From the free fireside of her unbought farmer —
   From her free laborer at his loom and wheel —
From the brown smith-shop, where, beneath the hammer,
             Rings the red steel —

From each and all, if God hath not forsaken
   Our land, and left us to an evil choice,
Loud as the summer thunderbolt shall waken
             A People's voice

Startling and stern! the Northern winds shall bear it
   Over Potomac's to St. Mary's wave;
And buried Freedom shall awake to hear it
             Within her grave.

O, let that voice go forth! The bondman sighing
   By Santee's wave, in Mississippi's cane,
Shall feel the hope, within his bosom dying,
             Revive again.

Let it go forth! The millions who are gazing
   Sadly upon us from afar, shall smile,
And unto God devout thanksgiving raising,
             Bless us the while.

O, for your ancient freedom, pure and holy,
 For the deliverance of a groaning earth,
For the wronged captive, bleeding, crushed, and lowly,
   Let it go forth!

Sons of the best of fathers! will ye falter
 With all they left ye perilled and at stake?
Ho! once again on Freedom's holy altar
   The fire awake!

Prayer-strengthened for the trial, come together,
 Put on the harness for the moral fight,
And, with the blessing of your Heavenly Father,
   MAINTAIN THE RIGHT!

THE CRISIS.

WRITTEN ON LEARNING THE TERMS OF THE TREATY WITH MEXICO.

ACROSS the Stony Mountains, o'er the desert's drouth and sand,
The circles of our empire touch the Western Ocean's strand;
From slumberous Timpanogos, to Gila, wild and free,
Flowing down from Neuva Leon to California's sea;
And from the mountains of the East, to Santa Rosa's shore,
The eagles of Mexitli shall beat the air no more.

O Vale of Rio Bravo! Let thy simple children weep;
Close watch about their holy fire let maids of Pecos keep;
Let Taos send her cry across Sierra Madre's pines,
And Algodones toll her bells amidst her corn and vines;
For lo! the pale land-seekers come, with eager eyes of gain,
Wide scattering, like the bison herds on broad Salada's plain.

Let Sacramento's herdsmen heed what sound, the winds bring
 down,
Of footsteps on the crisping snow, from cold Nevada's crown!
Full hot and fast the Saxon rides, with rein of travel slack,
And, bending o'er his saddle, leaves the sunrise at his back;
By many a lonely river, and gorge of fir and pine,
On many a wintry hill-top, his nightly camp-fires shine.

O countrymen and brothers! that land of lake and plain,
Of salt wastes alternating with valleys fat with grain;
Of mountains white with winter, looking downward, cold, serene,
On their feet with spring-vines tangled and lapped in softest geeen;
Swift through whose black volcanic gates, o'er many a sunny vale,
Wind-like the Arapahoe sweeps the bison's dusty trail!

Great spaces yet untravelled, great lakes whose mystic shores
The Saxon rifle never heard, nor dip of Saxon oars;
Great herds that wander all unwatched, wild steeds that none have
 tamed,
Strange fish in unknown streams, and birds the Saxon never
 named;
Deep mines, dark mountain crucibles, where Nature's chemic
 powers
Work out the Great Designer's will: — all these ye say are ours!

Forever ours! for good or ill, on us the burden lies;
God's balance, watched by angels, is hung across the skies.
Shall Justice, Truth, and Freedom, turn the poised and trembling
 scale?
Or shall the Evil triumph, and robber Wrong prevail?
Shall the broad land o'er which our flag in starry splendor waves,
Forego through us its freedom, and bear the tread of slaves?

The day is breaking in the East, of which the prophets told,
And brightens up the sky of Time the Christian Age of Gold:
Old Might to Right is yielding, battle blade to clerkly pen,
Earth's monarchs are her peoples, and her serfs stand up as men;
The isles rejoice together, in a day are nations born,
And the slave walks free in Tunis, and by Stamboul's Golden Horn!

Is this, O countrymen of mine ! a day for us to sow
The soil of new-gained empire with slavery's seeds of woe?
To feed with our fresh life-blood the old world's cast-off crime,
Dropped, like some monstrous early birth, from the tired lap of
    Time ?
To run anew the evil race the old lost nations ran,
And die like them of unbelief of God, and wrong of man?

Great Heaven! Is this our mission? End in this the prayers
    and tears,
The toil, the strife, the watchings of our younger, better years?
Still, as the old world rolls in light, shall ours in shadow turn,
A beamless Chaos, cursed of God, through outer darkness borne?
Where the far nations looked for light, a blackness in the air?
Where for words of hope they listened, the long wail of despair?

The Crisis presses on us; face to face with us it stands,
With solemn lips of question, like the Sphinx in Egypt's sands!
This day we fashion Destiny, our web of Fate we spin;
This day for all hereafter choose we holiness or sin;
Even now from starry Gerizim, or Ebal's cloudy crown,
We call the dews of blessing or the bolts of cursing down!

By all for which the martyrs bore their agony and shame;
By all the warning words of truth with which the prophets came;
By the Future which awaits us; by all the hopes which cast
Their faint and trembling beams across the blackness of the Past;
And by the blessed thought of Him who for Earth's freedom died,
O my people! O my brothers! let us choose the righteous side.

So shall the Northern pioneer go joyful on his way;
To wed Penobscot's waters to San Francisco's bay;
To make the rugged places smooth, and sow the vales with grain;
And bear, with Liberty and Law, the Bible in his train:
The mighty West shall bless the East, and sea shall answer sea,
And mountain unto mountain call: PRAISE GOD, FOR WE ARE
    FREE !

RANDOLPH OF ROANOKE.

O MOTHER Earth! upon thy lap
   Thy weary ones receiving,
And o'er them, silent as a dream,
   Thy grassy mantle weaving,
Fold softly in thy long embrace
   That heart so worn and broken,
And cool its pulse of fire beneath
   Thy shadows old and oaken.

Shut out from him the bitter word
   And serpent hiss of scorning;
Nor let the storms of yesterday
   Disturb his quiet morning.
Breathe over him forgetfulness
   Of all save deeds of kindness,
And, save to smiles of grateful eyes,
   Press down his lids in blindness.

There, where with living ear and eye
   He heard Potomac's flowing,
And, through his tall ancestral trees,
   Saw Autumn's sunset glowing,
He sleeps, — still looking to the West,
   Beneath the dark wood shadow,
As if he still would see the sun
   Sink down on wave and meadow.

Bard, Sage, and Tribune! — in himself
   All moods of mind contrasting, —
The tenderest wail of human woe,
   The scorn-like lightning blasting;

The pathos which from rival eyes
    Unwilling tears could summon,
The stinging taunt, the fiery burst
    Of hatred scarcely human!

Mirth, sparkling like a diamond shower,
    From lips of life-long sadness;
Clear picturings of majestic thought
    Upon a ground of madness;
And over all Romance and Song
    A classic beauty throwing,
And laurelled Clio at his side
    Her storied pages showing.

All parties feared him: each in turn
    Beheld its schemes disjointed,
As right or left his fatal glance
    And spectral finger pointed.
Sworn foe of Cant, he smote it down
    With trenchant wit unsparing,
And, mocking, rent with ruthless hand
    The robe Pretence was wearing.

Too honest or too proud to feign
    A love he never cherished,
Beyond Virginia's border line
    His patriotism perished.
While others hailed in distant skies
    Our eagle's dusky pinion,
He only saw the mountain bird
    Stoop o'er his Old Dominion!

Still through each change of fortune strange,
    Racked nerve, and brain all burning,
His loving faith in Mother-land
    Knew never shade of turning;
By Britain's lakes, by Neva's wave,
    Whatever sky was o'er him,
He heard her rivers' rushing sound,
    Her blue peaks rose before him.

He held his slaves, yet made withal
    No false and vain pretences,
Nor paid a lying priest to seek
    For scriptural defences.
His harshest words of proud rebuke,
    His bitterest taunt and scorning,
Fell fire-like on the Northern brow
    That bent to him in fawning.

He held his slaves : yet kept the while
    His reverence for the Human ;
In the dark vassals of his will
    He saw but Man and Woman !
No hunter of God's outraged poor
    His Roanoke valley entered ;
No trader in the souls of men
    Across his threshold ventured.

And when the old and wearied man
    Laid down for his last sleeping,
And at his side, a slave no more,
    His brother man stood weeping,
His latest thought, his latest breath,
    To Freedom's duty giving,
With failing tongue and trembling hand
    The dying blest the living.

O, never bore his ancient State
    A truer son or braver !
None trampling with a calmer scorn
    On foreign hate or favor.
He knew her faults, yet never stooped
    His proud and manly feeling
To poor excuses of the wrong
    Or meanness of concealing.

But none beheld with clearer eye
    The plague-spot o'er her spreading,
None heard more sure the steps of Doom
    Along her future treading.

For her as for himself he spake,
  When, his gaunt frame upbracing,
He traced with dying hand "REMORSE!"
  And perished in the tracing.

As from the grave where Henry sleeps,
  From Vernon's weeping willow,
And from the grassy pall which hides
  The Sage of Monticello,
So from the leaf-strewn burial-stone
  Of Randolph's lowly dwelling,
Virginia! o'er thy land of slaves
  A warning voice is swelling!

And hark! from thy deserted fields
  Are sadder warnings spoken,
From quenched hearths, where thy exiled sons
  Their household gods have broken.
The curse is on thee, — wolves for men,
  And briers for corn-sheaves giving!
O, more than all thy dead renown
  Were now one hero living!

THE ANGELS OF BUENA VISTA.

SPEAK and tell us, our Ximena, looking northward far away,
O'er the camp of the invaders, o'er the Mexican array,
Who is losing? who is winning? are they far or come they near?
Look abroad, and tell us, sister, whither rolls the storm we hear.

"Down the hills of Angostura still the storm of battle rolls;
Blood is flowing, men are dying; God have mercy on their souls!"

Who is losing ? who is winning ? — " Over hill and over plain,
I see but smoke of cannon clouding through the mountain rain."

Holy Mother! keep our brothers! Look, Ximena, look once more:
" Still I see the fearful whirlwind rolling darkly as before,
Bearing on, in strange confusion, friend and foeman, foot and horse,
Like some wild and troubled torrent sweeping down its mountain course."

Look forth once more, Ximena! " Ah! the smoke has rolled away;
And I see the Northern rifles gleaming down the ranks of gray.
Hark! that sudden blast of bugles! there the troop of Minon wheels;
There the Northern horses thunder, with the cannon at their heels.

" Jesu, pity! how it thickens! now retreat and now advance!
Right against the blazing cannon shivers Puebla's charging lance!
Down they go, the brave young riders; horse and foot together fall;
Like a ploughshare in the fallow, through them ploughs the Northern ball."

Nearer came the storm and nearer, rolling fast and frightful on:
Speak, Ximena, speak and tell us, who has lost, and who has won?
" Alas! alas! I know not; friend and foe together fall,
O'er the dying rush the living: pray, my sisters, for them all!"

" Lo! the wind the smoke is lifting: Blessed Mother, save my brain!
I can see the wounded crawling slowly out from heaps of slain.
Now they stagger, blind and bleeding; now they fall, and strive to rise;
Hasten, sisters, haste and save them, lest they die before our eyes!"

" O my heart's love! O my dear one! lay thy poor head on my knee;
Dost thou know the lips that kiss thee? Canst thou hear me? canst thou see?
O my husband, brave and gentle! O my Bernal, look once more
On the blessed cross before thee! mercy! mercy! all is o'er!"

Dry thy tears, my poor Ximena; lay thy dear one down to rest;
Let his hands be meekly folded, lay the cross upon his breast;
Let his dirge be sung hereafter, and his funeral masses said;
To-day, thou poor bereaved one, the living ask thy aid.

Close beside her, faintly moaning, fair and young, a soldier lay,
Torn with shot and pierced with lances, bleeding slow his life away;
But, as tenderly before him, the lorn Ximena knelt,
She saw the Northern eagle shining on his pistol-belt.

With a stifled cry of horror straight she turned away her head;
With a sad and bitter feeling looked she back upon her dead;
But she heard the youth's low moaning, and his struggling breath
    of pain,
And she raised the cooling water to his parching lips again.

Whispered low the dying soldier, pressed her hand and faintly
    smiled:
Was that pitying face his mother's? did she watch beside her child?
All his stranger words with meaning her woman's heart supplied;
With her kiss upon his forehead, "Mother!" murmured he, and
    died!

"A bitter curse upon them, poor boy, who led thee forth,
From some gentle, sad-eyed mother, weeping, lonely, in the North!"
Spake the mournful Mexic woman, as she laid him with her dead,
And turned to soothe the living, and bind the wounds which bled.

Look forth once more, Ximena! "Like a cloud before the wind
Rolls the battle down the mountains, leaving blood and death be-
    hind;
Ah! they plead in vain for mercy; in the dust the wounded strive;
Hide your faces, holy angels! O, thou Christ of God, forgive!"

Sink, O Night, among thy mountains! let the cool, gray shadows
    fall;
Dying brothers, fighting demons, drop thy curtain over all!
Through the thickening winter twilight, wide apart the battle rolled,
In its sheath the sabre rested, and the cannon's lips grew cold.

But the noble Mexic women still their holy task pursued,
Through that long, dark night of sorrow, worn and faint and
    lacking food;
Over weak and suffering brothers, with a tender care they hung,
And the dying foeman blessed them in a strange and Northern
    tongue.

Not wholly lost, O Father! is this evil world of ours;
Upward, through its blood and ashes, spring afresh the Eden
    flowers;
From its smoking hell of battle, Love and Pity send their prayer,
And still thy white-winged angels hover dimly in our air!

DEMOCRACY.

"All things whatsoever ye would that men should do to you, do ye even
so to them." — *Matthew* vii. 12.

BEARER of Freedom's holy light,
    Breaker of Slavery's chain and rod,
The foe of all which pains the sight,
    Or wounds the generous ear of God!

Beautiful yet thy temples rise,
    Though there profaning gifts are thrown;
And fires unkindled of the skies
    Are glaring round thy altar-stone.

Still sacred, — though thy name be breathed
    By those whose hearts thy truth deride;
And garlands, plucked from thee, are wreathed
    Around the haughty brows of Pride.

DEMOCRACY.

O, ideal of my boyhood's time!
    The faith in which my father stood,
Even when the sons of Lust and Crime
    Had stained thy peaceful courts with blood!

Still to those courts my footsteps turn,
    For, through the mists which darken there,
I see the flame of Freedom burn, —
    The Kebla of the patriot's prayer!

The generous feeling, pure and warm,
    Which owns the rights of *all* divine —
The pitying heart — the helping arm —
    The prompt self-sacrifice — are thine.

Beneath thy broad, impartial eye,
    How fade the lines of caste and birth!
How equal in their suffering lie
    The groaning multitudes of earth!

Still to a stricken brother true,
    Whatever clime hath nurtured him;
As stooped to heal the wounded Jew
    The worshipper of Gerizim.

By misery unrepelled, unawed
    By pomp or power, thou see'st a MAN
In prince or peasant — slave or lord —
    Pale priest, or swarthy artisan.

Through all disguise, form, place, or name,
    Beneath the flaunting robes of sin,
Through poverty and squalid shame,
    Thou lookest on *the man* within.

On man, as man, retaining yet,
    Howe'er debased, and soiled, and dim,
The crown upon his forehead set, —
    The immortal gift of God to him.

And there is reverence in thy look;
  For that frail form which mortals wear
The Spirit of the Holiest took,
  And veiled his perfect brightness there.

Not from the shallow babbling fount
  Of vain philosophy thou art;
He who of old on Syria's mount
  Thrilled, warmed, by turns, the listener's heart,

In holy words which cannot die,
  In thoughts which angels leaned to know,
Proclaimed thy message from on high, —
  Thy mission to a world of woe.

That voice's echo hath not died!
  From the blue lake of Galilee,
And Tabor's lonely mountain side,
  It calls a struggling world to thee.

Thy name and watchword o'er this land
  I hear in every breeze that stirs,
And round a thousand altars stand
  Thy banded party worshippers.

Not to these altars of a day,
  At party's call, my gift I bring;
But on thy olden shrine I lay
  A freeman's dearest offering: —

The voiceless utterance of his will, —
  His pledge to Freedom and to Truth,
That manhood's heart remembers still
  The homage of his generous youth.

Election Day, 1843.

THY WILL BE DONE.

WE see not, know not; all our way
  Is night, — with Thee alone is day:
From out the torrent's troubled drift,
Above the storm our prayers we lift,
      Thy will be done!

The flesh may fail, the heart may faint,
But who are we to make complaint,
Or dare to plead, in times like these,
The weakness of our love of ease?
      Thy will be done!

We take with solemn thankfulness
Our burden up, nor ask it less,
And count it joy that even we
May suffer, serve, or wait, for Thee,
      Whose will be done!

Though dim as yet in tint and line,
We trace Thy picture's wise design,
And thank Thee that our age supplies
Its dark relief of sacrifice.
      Thy will be done!

And if, in our unworthiness,
Thy sacrificial wine we press;
If from Thy ordeal's heated bars
Our feet are seamed with crimson scars,
      Thy will be done!

If, for the age to come, this hour
Of trial hath vicarious power,

And, blest by Thee, our present pain
Be Liberty's eternal gain,
   Thy will be done!

Strike, Thou the Master, we Thy keys,
The anthem of the destinies!
The minor of Thy loftier strain,
Our hearts shall breathe the old refrain,
   Thy will be done!

"EIN FESTE BURG IST UNSER GOTT."

(LUTHER'S HYMN.)

WE wait beneath the furnace-blast
   The pangs of transformation;
Not painlessly doth God recast
   And mould anew the nation.
      Hot burns the fire
      Where wrongs expire;
      Nor spares the hand
      That from the land
Uproots the ancient evil.

The hand-breadth cloud the sages feared
   Its bloody rain is dropping;
The poison plant the fathers spared
   All else is overtopping.
      East, West, South, North,
      It curses the earth;
      All justice dies,
      And fraud and lies
Live only in its shadow.

"EIN FESTE BURG IST UNSER GOTT."

What gives the wheat-field blades of steel?
What points the rebel cannon?
What sets the roaring rabble's heel
   On the old star-spangled pennon?
     What breaks the oath
     Of the men o' the South?
     What whets the knife
     For the Union's life? —
Hark to the answer: Slavery!

Then waste no blows on lesser foes
   In strife unworthy freemen.
God lifts to-day the veil, and shows
   The features of the demon!
     O North and South,
     Its victims both,
     Can ye not cry,
     "Let slavery die!"
And union find in freedom?

What though the cast-out spirit tear
   The nation in his going?
We who have shared the guilt must share
   The pang of his o'erthrowing!
     Whate'er the loss,
     Whate'er the cross,
     Shall they complain
     Of present pain
Who trust in God's hereafter?

For who that leans on His right arm
   Was ever yet forsaken?
What righteous cause can suffer harm
   If He its part has taken?
     Though wild and loud
     And dark the cloud,
     Behind its folds
     His hand upholds
The calm sky of to-morrow!

Above the maddening cry for blood,
    Above the wild war-drumming,
Let Freedom's voice be heard, with good
    The evil overcoming.
        Give prayer and purse
        To stay the Curse
        Whose wrong we share,
        Whose shame we bear,
Whose end shall gladden Heaven!

In vain the bells of war shall ring
    Of triumphs and revenges,
While still is spared the evil thing
    That severs and estranges.
        But blest the ear
        That yet shall hear
        The jubilant bell
        That rings the knell
Of Slavery forever!

Then let the selfish lip be dumb,
    And hushed the breath of sighing;
Before the joy of peace must come
    The pains of purifying.
        God give us grace
        Each in his place
        To bear his lot,
        And, murmuring not,
Endure and wait and labor!

ASTRÆA AT THE CAPITOL.

ABOLITION OF SLAVERY IN THE DISTRICT OF COLUMBIA, 1862.

WHEN first I saw our banner wave
    Above the nation's council-hall,
    I heard beneath its marble wall
The clanking fetters of the slave!

In the foul market-place I stood,
    And saw the Christian mother sold,
    And childhood with its locks of gold,
Blue-eyed and fair with Saxon blood.

I shut my eyes, I held my breath,
    And, smothering down the wrath and shame
    That set my Northern blood aflame,
Stood silent — where to speak was death.

Beside me gloomed the prison-cell
    Where wasted one in slow decline
    For uttering simple words of mine,
And loving freedom all too well.

The flag that floated from the dome
    Flapped menace in the morning air;
    I stood a perilled stranger where
The human broker made his home.

For crime was virtue: Gown and Sword
    And Law their threefold sanction gave,
    And to the quarry of the slave
Went hawking with our symbol-bird.

On the oppressor's side was power;
   And yet I knew that every wrong,
   However old, however strong,
But waited God's avenging hour.

I knew that truth would crush the lie, —
   Somehow, sometime, the end would be;
   Yet scarcely dared I hope to see
The triumph with my mortal eye.

But now I see it! In the sun
   A free flag floats from yonder dome,
   And at the nation's hearth and home
The justice long delayed is done.

Not as we hoped, in calm of prayer,
   The message of deliverance comes,
   But heralded by roll of drums
On waves of battle-troubled air! —

Midst sounds that madden and appall,
   The song that Bethlehem's shepherds knew!
   The harp of David melting through
The demon-agonies of Saul!

Not as we hoped; — but what are we?
   Above our broken dreams and plans
   God lays, with wiser hand than man's,
The corner-stones of liberty.

I cavil not with Him: the voice
   That freedom's blessed gospel tells
   Is sweet to me as silver bells,
Rejoicing! — yea, I will rejoice!

Dear friends still toiling in the sun, —
   Ye dearer ones who, gone before,
   Are watching from the eternal shore
The slow work by your hands begun, —

Rejoice with me! The chastening rod
  Blossoms with love; the furnace heat
  Grows cool beneath His blessed feet
Whose form is as the Son of God!

Rejoice! Our Marah's bitter springs
  Are sweetened; on our ground of grief
  Rise day by day in strong relief
The prophecies of better things.

Rejoice in hope! The day and night
  Are one with God, and one with them
  Who see by faith the cloudy hem
Of Judgment fringed with Mercy's light!

THE PASS OF THE SIERRA.

ALL night above their rocky bed
  They saw the stars march slow;
The wild Sierra overhead,
  The desert's death below.

The Indian from his lodge of bark,
  The gray bear from his den,
Beyond their camp-fire's wall of dark,
  Glared on the mountain men.

Still upward turned, with anxious strain,
  Their leader's sleepless eye,
Where splinters of the mountain chain
  Stood black against the sky.

The night waned slow: at last, a glow,
  A gleam of sudden fire,

Shot up behind the walls of snow,
    And tipped each icy spire.

" Up, men ! " he cried, " yon rocky cone,
    To-day, please God, we 'll pass,
And look from Winter's frozen throne
    On Summer's flowers and grass ! "

They set their faces to the blast,
    They trod th' eternal snow,
And faint, worn, bleeding, hailed at last
    The promised land below.

Behind, they saw the snow-cloud tossed
  By many an icy horn ;
Before, warm valleys, wood-embossed,
  And green with vines and corn.

They left the Winter at their backs
  To flap his baffled wing,
And downward, with the cataracts,
  Leaped to the lap of Spring.

Strong leader of that mountain band
  Another task remains,
To break from Slavery's desert land
  A path to Freedom's plains.

The winds are wild, the way is drear
  Yet, flashing through the night,
Lo ! icy ridge and rocky spear
  Blaze out in morning light !

Rise up, FREMONT ! and go before ;
  The Hour must have its Man ;
Put on the hunting-shirt once more,
  And lead in Freedom's van !

8th mo., 1856.

THE BATTLE AUTUMN OF 1862.

THE flags of war like storm-birds fly,
  The charging trumpets blow ;
Yet rolls no thunder in the sky,
  No earthquake strives below.

And, calm and patient, Nature keeps
  Her ancient promise well,
Though o'er her bloom and greenness sweeps
  The battle's breath of hell.

And still she walks in golden hours
    Through harvest-happy farms,
And still she wears her fruits and flowers
    Like jewels on her arms.

What mean the gladness of the plain,
    This joy of eve and morn,
The mirth that shakes the beard of grain
    And yellow locks of corn?

Ah! eyes may well be full of tears,
    And hearts with hate are hot;
But even-paced come round the years,
    And Nature changes not.

She meets with smiles our bitter grief,
    With songs our groans of pain;
She mocks with tint of flower and leaf
    The war-field's crimson stain.

Still, in the cannon's pause, we hear
    Her sweet thanksgiving-psalm;
Too near to God for doubt or fear,
    She shares th' eternal calm.

She knows the seed lies safe below
    The fires that blast and burn;
For all the tears of blood we sow
    She waits the rich return.

She sees with clearer eye than ours
    The good of suffering born, —
The hearts that blossom like her flowers,
    And ripen like her corn.

O, give to us, in times like these,
    The vision of her eyes;
And make her fields and fruited trees
    Our golden prophecies!

O, give to us her finer ear!
  Above this stormy din,
We too would hear the bells of cheer
  Ring peace and freedom in!

MITHRIDATES AT CHIOS.

KNOW'ST thou, O slave-cursed land!
  How, when the Chian's cup of guilt
    Was full to overflow, there came
    God's justice in the sword of flame
  That, red with slaughter to its hilt,
Blazed in the Cappadocian victor's hand?

  The heavens are still and far;
  But, not unheard of awful Jove,
    The sighing of the island slave
    Was answered, when the Ægean wave
  The keels of Mithridates clove,
And the vines shrivelled in the breath of war.

  "Robbers of Chios! hark,"
  The victor cried, "to Heaven's decree!
    Pluck your last cluster from the vine,
    Drain your last cup of Chian wine;
  Slaves of your slaves, your doom shall be,
In Colchian mines by Phasis rolling dark."

  Then rose the long lament
  From the hoar sea-god's dusky caves:
    The priestess rent her hair and cried,
    "Woe! woe! The gods are sleepless-eyed!"
  And, chained and scourged, the slaves of slaves,
The lords of Chios into exile went.

"The gods at last pay well,"
So Hellas sang her taunting song,
"The fisher in his net is caught,
The Chian hath his master bought";
And isle from isle, with laughter long,
Took up and sped the mocking parable.

Once more the slow, dumb years
Bring their avenging cycle round,
And, more than Hellas taught of old,
Our wiser lesson shall be told,
Of slaves uprising, freedom-crowned,
To break, not wield, the scourge wet with their blood and tears.

THE PROCLAMATION.

SAINT PATRICK, slave to Milcho of the herds
Of Ballymena, wakened with these words:
"Arise, and flee
Out from the land of bondage, and be free!"

Glad as a soul in pain, who hears from heaven
The angels singing of his sins forgiven,
And, wondering, sees
His prison opening to their golden keys,

He rose a man who laid him down a slave,
Shook from his locks the ashes of the grave,
And outward trod
Into the glorious liberty of God.

He cast the symbols of his shame away;
And, passing where the sleeping Milcho lay,
Though back and limb
Smarted with wrong, he prayed, "God pardon him!"

So went he forth: but in God's time he came
To light on Uilline's hills a holy flame;
    And, dying, gave
The land a saint that lost him as a slave.

O dark, sad millions, patiently and dumb
Waiting for God, your hour, at last, has come,
    And freedom's song
Breaks the long silence of your night of wrong!

Arise and flee! shake off the vile restraint
Of ages; but, like Ballymena's saint,
    The oppressor spare,
Heap only on his head the coals of prayer.

Go forth, like him! like him return again,
To bless the land whereon in bitter pain
    Ye toiled at first,
And heal with freedom what your slavery cursed.

AT PORT ROYAL.

THE tent-lights glimmer on the land,
  The ship-lights on the sea;
The night-wind smooths with drifting sand
  Our track on lone Tybee.

At last our grating keels outslide,
  Our good boats forward swing;
And while we ride the land-locked tide,
  Our negroes row and sing.

AT PORT ROYAL.

For dear the bondman holds his gifts
  Of music and of song:
The gold that kindly Nature sifts
  Among his sands of wrong;

The power to make his toiling days
  And poor home-comforts please;
The quaint relief of mirth that plays
  With sorrow's minor keys.

Another glow than sunset's fire
  Has filled the West with light,
Where field and garner, barn and byre
  Are blazing through the night.

The land is wild with fear and hate,
  The rout runs mad and fast;
From hand to hand, from gate to gate,
  The flaming brand is passed.

The lurid glow falls strong across
  Dark faces broad with smiles:
Not theirs the terror, hate, and loss
  That fire yon blazing piles.

With oar-strokes timing to their song,
  They weave in simple lays
The pathos of remembered wrong,
  The hope of better days, —

The triumph-note that Miriam sung,
  The joy of uncaged birds:
Softening with Afric's mellow tongue
  Their broken Saxon words.

SONG OF THE NEGRO BOATMEN.

O, praise an' tanks! De Lord he come
  To set de people free;
An' massa tink it day ob doom,
  An' we ob jubilee.

NATIONAL LYRICS.

De Lord dat heap de Red-Sea waves
  He jus' as 'trong as den;
He say de word: we las' night slaves;
  To-day, de Lord's freemen.
    De yam will grow, de cotton blow,
      We 'll hab de rice an' corn;
    O nebber you fear, if nebber you hear
      De driver blow his horn!

Ole massa on he trabbels gone;
  He leaf de land behind:
De Lord's breff blow him furder on,
  Like corn-shuck in de wind.
We own de hoe, we own de plough,
  We own de hands dat hold;
We sell de pig, we sell de cow,
  But nebber chile be sold.
    De yam will grow, de cotton blow,
      We 'll hab de rice an' corn:
    O nebber you fear, if nebber you hear
      De driver blow his horn!

We pray de Lord: he gib us signs
  Dat some day we be free;
De Norf-wind tell it to de pines,
  De wild-duck to de sea;
We tink it when de church-bell ring,
  We dream it in de dream;
De rice-bird mean it when he sing,
  De eagle when he scream.
    De yam will grow, de cotton blow,
      We 'll hab de rice an' corn:
    O nebber you fear, if nebber you hear
      De driver blow his horn!

We know de promise nebber fail,
  An' nebber lie de word;
So like de 'postles in de jail,
  We waited for de Lord:

AT PORT ROYAL.

An' now he open ebery door,
  An' trow away de key;
He tink we lub him so before,
  We lub him better free.
    De yam will grow, de cotton blow,
      He 'll gib de rice an' corn:
    O nebber you fear, if nebber you hear
      De driver blow his horn!

So sing our dusky gondoliers;
  And, with a secret pain,
And smiles that seem akin to tears,
  We hear the wild refrain.

We dare not share the negro's trust,
  Nor yet his hope deny;
We only know that God is just,
  And every wrong shall die.

Rude seems the song; each swarthy face,
  Flame-lighted, ruder still:
We start to think that hapless race
  Must shape our good or ill;

That laws of changeless justice bind
  Oppressor with oppressed;
And, close as sin and suffering joined,
  We march to Fate abreast.

Sing on, poor hearts! your chant shall be
  Our sign of blight or bloom, —
The Vala-song of Liberty,
  Or death-rune of our doom!

ICHABOD!

So fallen! so lost! the light withdrawn
    Which once he wore!
The glory from his gray hairs gone
    Forevermore!

Revile him not, — the Tempter hath
    A snare for all;
And pitying tears, not scorn and wrath,
    Befit his fall!

O, dumb be passion's stormy rage,
    When he who might
Have lighted up and led his age
    Falls back in night!

Scorn! would the angels laugh, to mark
    A bright soul driven,
Fiend-goaded, down the endless dark,
    From hope and heaven?

Let not the land, once proud of him,
    Insult him now,
Nor brand with deeper shame his dim,
    Dishonored brow.

But let its humbled sons, instead,
    From sea to lake,
A long lament, as for the dead,
    In sadness make.

Of all we loved and honored, naught
    Save power remains, —
A fallen angel's pride of thought,
    Still strong in chains.

All else is gone; from those great eyes
    The soul has fled:
When faith is lost, when honor dies,
    The man is dead!

Then, pay the reverence of old days
    To his dead fame;
Walk backward, with averted gaze,
    And hide the shame!

OUR STATE.

THE South-land boasts its teeming cane,
    The prairied West its heavy grain,
And sunset's radiant gates unfold
On rising marts and sands of gold!

Rough, bleak and hard, our little State
Is scant of soil, of limits strait;
Her yellow sands are sands alone,
Her only mines are ice and stone!

From Autumn frost to April rain,
Too long her winter woods complain;
From budding flower to falling leaf,
Her summer time is all too brief.

Yet, on her rocks, and on her sands,
And wintry hills, the school-house stands,
And what her rugged soil denies,
The harvest of the mind supplies.

The riches of the commonwealth
Are free, strong minds, and hearts of health;
And more to her than gold or grain,
The cunning hand and cultured brain.

For well she keeps her ancient stock,
The stubborn strength of Pilgrim Rock;
And still maintains, with milder laws,
And clearer light, the Good Old Cause!

Nor heeds the sceptic's puny hands,
While near her school the church-spire stands;
Nor fears the blinded bigot's rule,
While near her church-spire stands the school!

STANZAS FOR THE TIMES.

1850.

THE evil days have come, — the poor
    Are made a prey;
Bar up the hospitable door,
Put out the fire-lights, point no more
    The wanderer's way.

For Pity now is crime; the chain
    Which binds our States
Is melted at her hearth in twain,
Is rusted by her tears' soft rain:
    Close up her gates.

Our Union, like a glacier stirred
    By voice below,
Or bell of kine, or wing of bird,
A beggar's crust, a kindly word
    May overthrow!

Poor, whispering tremblers! — yet we boast
    Our blood and name;
Bursting its century-bolted frost,
Each gray cairn on the Northman's coast
    Cries out for shame!

STANZAS FOR THE TIMES.

O for the open firmament,
    The prairie free,
The desert hillside, cavern-rent,
The Pawnee's lodge, the Arab's tent,
    The Bushman's tree!

Than web of Persian loom most rare,
    Or soft divan,
Better the rough rock, bleak and bare,
Or hollow tree, which man may share
    With suffering man.

I hear a voice: "Thus saith the Law,
    Let Love be dumb;
Clasping her liberal hands in awe,
Let sweet-lipped Charity withdraw
    From hearth and home."

I hear another voice: "The poor
    Are thine to feed;
Turn not the outcast from thy door,
Nor give to bonds and wrong once more
    Whom God hath freed."

Dear Lord! between that law and thee
    No choice remains;
Yet not untrue to man's decree,
Though spurning its rewards, is he
    Who bears its pains.

Not mine Sedition's trumpet-blast
    And threatening word;
I read the lesson of the Past,
That firm endurance wins at last
    More than the sword.

O, clear-eyed Faith, and Patience, thou
    So calm and strong!
Lend strength to weakness, teach us how
The sleepless eyes of God look through
    This night of wrong!

A SABBATH SCENE.

S CARCE had the solemn Sabbath-bell
   Ceased quivering in the steeple,
Scarce had the parson to his desk
   Walked stately through his people,

A SABBATH SCENE.

When down the summer shaded street
　A wasted female figure,
With dusky brow and naked feet,
　Came rushing wild and eager.

She saw the white spire through the trees,
　She heard the sweet hymn swelling;
O, pitying Christ! a refuge give
　That poor one in thy dwelling!

Like a scared fawn before the hounds,
　Right up the aisle she glided,
While close behind her, whip in hand,
　A lank-haired hunter strided.

She raised a keen and bitter cry,
　To Heaven and Earth appealing; —
Were manhood's generous pulses dead?
　Had woman's heart no feeling?

A score of stout hands rose between
　The hunter and the flying;
Age clenched his staff, and maiden eyes
　Flashed tearful, yet defying.

"Who dares profane this house and day?"
　Cried out the angry pastor.
"Why, bless your soul, the wench's a slave,
　And I'm her lord and master!

"I've law and gospel on my side,
　And who shall dare refuse me?"
Down came the parson, bowing low,
　"My good sir, pray excuse me!

"Of course I know your right divine
　To own and work and whip her;
Quick, deacon, throw that Polyglot
　Before the wench, and trip her!"

Plump dropped the holy tome, and o'er
    Its sacred pages stumbling,
Bound hand and foot, a slave once more,
    The hapless wretch lay trembling.

I saw the parson tie the knots,
    The while his flock addressing,
The Scriptural claims of slavery
    With text on text impressing.

"Although," said he, "on Sabbath day,
    All secular occupations
Are deadly sins, we must fulfil
    Our moral obligations:

"And this commends itself as one
    To every conscience tender;
As Paul sent back Onesimus,
    My Christian friends, we send her!"

Shriek rose on shriek, — the Sabbath air
    Her wild cries tore asunder;
I listened, with hushed breath, to hear
    God answering with his thunder!

All still! — the very altar's cloth
    Had smothered down her shrieking,
And, dumb, she turned from face to face,
    For human pity seeking!

I saw her dragged along the aisle,
    Her shackles harshly clanking;
I heard the parson, over all,
    The Lord devoutly thanking!

My brain took fire: "Is this," I cried,
    "The end of prayer and preaching?
Then down with pulpit, down with priest,
    And give us Nature's teaching!

"Foul shame and scorn be on ye all
    Who turn the good to evil,
And steal the Bible from the Lord,
    To give it to the Devil!

"Than garbled text or parchment law
    I own a statute higher;
And God is true, though every book
    And every man's a liar!"

Just then I felt the deacon's hand
    In wrath my coat-tail seize on;
I heard the priest cry "Infidel!"
    The lawyer mutter "Treason!"

I started up, — where now were church,
    Slave, master, priest and people?
I only heard the supper-bell,
    Instead of clanging steeple.

But, on the open window's sill,
    O'er which the white blooms drifted,
The pages of a good old Book
    The wind of summer lifted.

And flower and vine, like angel wings
    Around the Holy Mother,
Waved softly there, as if God's truth
    And Mercy kissed each other.

And freely from the cherry-bough
    Above the casement swinging,
With golden bosom to the sun,
    The oriole was singing.

As bird and flower made plain of old
    The lesson of the Teacher,
So now I heard the written Word
    Interpreted by Nature!

For to my ear methought the breeze
   Bore Freedom's blessed word on;
THUS SAITH THE LORD: BREAK EVERY YOKE,
UNDO THE HEAVY BURDEN!

RANTOUL.

ONE day, along the electric wire
   His manly word for Freedom sped;
We came next morn: that tongue of fire
   Said only, "He who spake is dead!"

Dead! while his voice was living yet,
   In echoes round the pillared dome!
Dead! while his blotted page lay wet
   With themes of state and loves of home!

Dead! in that crowning grace of time,
   That triumph of life's zenith hour!
Dead! while we watched his manhood's prime
   Break from the slow bud into flower!

Dead! he so great, and strong, and wise,
   While the mean thousands yet drew breath;
How deepened, through that dread surprise,
   The mystery and the awe of death!

From the high place whereon our votes
   Had borne him, clear, calm, earnest, fell
His first words, like the prelude notes
   Of some great anthem yet to swell.

We seemed to see our flag unfurled,
   Our champion waiting in his place
For the last battle of the world, —
   The Armageddon of the race.

Through him we hoped to speak the word
    Which wins the freedom of a land;
And lift, for human right, the sword
    Which dropped from Hampden's dying hand.

For he had sat at Sidney's feet,
    And walked with Pym and Vane apart;
And, through the centuries, felt the beat
    Of Freedom's march in Cromwell's heart.

He knew the paths the worthies held,
    Where England's best and wisest trod:
And, lingering, drank the springs that welled
    Beneath the touch of Milton's rod.

No wild enthusiast of the right,
    Self-poised and clear, he showed alway
The coolness of his northern night,
    The ripe repose of autumn's day.

His steps were slow, yet forward still
    He pressed where others paused or failed;
The calm star clomb with constant will, —
    The restless meteor flashed and paled!

Skilled in its subtlest wile, he knew
    And owned the higher ends of Law;
Still rose majestic on his view
    The awful Shape the schoolman saw.

Her home the heart of God; her voice
    The choral harmonics whereby
The stars, through all their spheres, rejoice,
    The rhythmic rule of earth and sky!

We saw his great powers misapplied
    To poor ambitions; yet, through all,
We saw him take the weaker side,
    And right the wronged, and free the thrall.

Now, looking o'er the frozen North
    For one like him in word and act,
To call her old, free spirit forth,
    And give her faith the life of fact, —

To break her party bonds of shame,
    And labor with the zeal of him
To make the Democratic name
    Of Liberty the synonyme, —

We sweep the land from hill to strand,
    We seek the strong, the wise, the brave,
And, sad of heart, return to stand
    In silence by a new-made grave!

There, where his breezy hills of home
    Look out upon his sail-white seas,
The sounds of winds and waters come,
    And shape themselves to words like these: —

"Why, murmuring, mourn that he, whose power
    Was lent to Party over-long,
Heard the still whisper at the hour
    He set his foot on Party wrong?

"The human life that closed so well
    No lapse of folly now can stain;
The lips whence Freedom's protest fell
    No meaner thought can now profane.

"Mightier than living voice his grave
    That lofty protest utters o'er;
Through roaring wind and smiting wave
    It speaks his hate of wrong once more.

"Men of the North! your weak regret
    Is wasted here; arise and pay
To freedom and to him your debt,
    By following where he led the way!"

BROWN OF OSSAWATOMIE.

JOHN BROWN OF OSSAWATOMIE spake on his dying day:
"I will not have to shrive my soul a priest in Slavery's pay.
But let some poor slave-mother whom I have striven to free,
With her children from the gallows-stair put up a prayer for me!"

John Brown of Ossawatomie, they led him out to die;
And lo! a poor slave-mother with her little child pressed nigh.
Then the bold, blue eye grew tender, and the old harsh face grew mild,
As he stooped between the jeering ranks and kissed the negro's child!

The shadows of his stormy life that moment fell apart;
And they who blamed the bloody hand forgave the loving heart.
That kiss from all its guilty means redeemed the good intent,
And round the grisly fighter's hair the martyr's aureole bent!

Perish with him the folly that seeks through evil good!
Long live the generous purpose unstained with human blood!
Not the raid of midnight terror, but the thought which underlies;
Not the borderer's pride of daring, but the Christian's sacrifice.

Never more may yon Blue Ridges the Northern rifle hear,
Nor see the light of blazing homes flash on the negro's spear.
But let the free-winged angel Truth their guarded passes scale,
To teach that right is more than might, and justice more than mail!

So vainly shall Virginia set her battle in array;
In vain her trampling squadrons knead the winter snow with clay.
She may strike the pouncing eagle, but she dares not harm the dove;
And every gate she bars to Hate shall open wide to Love!

THE RENDITION.

I HEARD the train's shrill whistle call,
   I saw an earnest look beseech,
  And rather by that look than speech
My neighbor told me all.

And, as I thought of Liberty
   Marched handcuffed down that sworded street,
   The solid earth beneath my feet
Reeled fluid as the sea.

I felt a sense of bitter loss, —
    Shame, tearless grief, and stifling wrath,
    And loathing fear, as if my path
A serpent stretched across.

All love of home, all pride of place,
    All generous confidence and trust,
    Sank smothering in that deep disgust
And anguish of disgrace.

Down on my native hills of June,
    And home's green quiet, hiding all,
    Fell sudden darkness, like the fall
Of midnight upon noon!

And Law, an unloosed maniac, strong,
    Blood-drunken, through the blackness trod,
    Hoarse-shouting in the ear of God
The blasphemy of wrong.

"O Mother, from thy memories proud,
    Thy old renown, dear Commonwealth,
    Lend this dead air a breeze of health,
And smite with stars this cloud.

"Mother of Freedom, wise and brave,
    Rise awful in thy strength," I said;
    Ah, me! I spake but to the dead;
I stood upon her grave!

6th mo., 1854.

LINES,

ON THE PASSAGE OF THE BILL TO PROTECT THE RIGHTS AND LIB-
ERTIES OF THE PEOPLE OF THE STATE AGAINST THE FUGITIVE
SLAVE ACT.

I SAID I stood upon thy grave,
    My Mother State, when last the moon
    Of blossoms clomb the skies of June.

And, scattering ashes on my head,
  I wore, undreaming of relief,
  The sackcloth of thy shame and grief.

Again that moon of blossoms shines
  On leaf and flower and folded wing,
  And thou hast risen with the spring!

Once more thy strong maternal arms
  Are round about thy children flung, —
  A lioness that guards her young!

No threat is on thy closéd lips,
  But in thine eye a power to smite
  The mad wolf backward from its light.

Southward the baffled robber's track
  Henceforth runs only; hereaway,
  The fell lycanthrope finds no prey.

Henceforth, within thy sacred gates,
  His first low howl shall downward draw
  The thunder of thy righteous law.

Not mindless of thy trade and gain,
  But, acting on the wiser plan,
  Thou 'rt grown conservative of man.

So shalt thou clothe with life the hope,
  Dream-painted on the sightless eyes
  Of him who sang of Paradise, —

The vision of a Christian man,
  In virtue as in stature great,
  Embodied in a Christian State.

And thou, amidst thy sisterhood
  Forbearing long, yet standing fast,
  Shalt win their grateful thanks at last;

When North and South shall strive no more,
  And all their feuds and fears be lost
  In Freedom's holy Pentecost.

6th mo., 1855.

THE POOR VOTER ON ELECTION DAY.

THE proudest now is but my peer,
    The highest not more high;
To-day, of all the weary year,
    A king of men am I.
To-day, alike are great and small,
    The nameless and the known;

My palace is the people's hall,
  The ballot-box my throne!

Who serves to-day upon the list
  Beside the served shall stand;
Alike the brown and wrinkled fist,
  The gloved and dainty hand!
The rich is level with the poor,
  The weak is strong to-day;
And sleekest broadcloth counts no more
  Than homespun frock of gray.

To-day let pomp and vain pretence
  My stubborn right abide;
I set a plain man's common sense
  Against the pedant's pride.
To-day shall simple manhood try
  The strength of gold and land;
The wide world has not wealth to buy
  The power in my right hand!

While there 's a grief to seek redress,
  Or balance to adjust,
Where weighs our living manhood less
  Than Mammon's vilest dust, —
While there 's a right to need my vote,
  A wrong to sweep away,
Up! clouted knee and ragged coat!
  A man 's a man to-day!

THE EVE OF ELECTION.

FROM gold to gray
  Our mild sweet day
Of Indian Summer fades too soon;
  But tenderly
  Above the sea
Hangs, white and calm, the Hunter's moon.

THE EVE OF ELECTION.

  In its pale fire
  The village spire
Shows like the zodiac's spectral lance;
  The painted walls
  Whereon it falls
Transfigured stand in marble trance!

  O'er fallen leaves
  The west wind grieves,
Yet comes a seed-time round again;
  And morn shall see
  The State sown free
With baleful tares or healthful grain.

  Along the street
  The shadows meet
Of Destiny, whose hands conceal
  The moulds of fate
  That shape the State,
And make or mar the common weal.

  Around I see
  The powers that be;
I stand by Empire's primal springs;
  And princes meet
  In every street,
And hear the tread of uncrowned kings!

  Hark! through the crowd
  The laugh runs loud,
Beneath the sad, rebuking moon.
  God save the land
  A careless hand
May shake or swerve ere morrow's noon!

  No jest is this;
  One cast amiss
May blast the hope of Freedom's year.
  O, take me where
  Are hearts of prayer,
And foreheads bowed in reverent fear!

Not lightly fall
Beyond recall
The written scrolls a breath can float;
The crowning fact,
The kingliest act
Of Freedom, is the freeman's vote!

For pearls that gem
A diadem
The diver in the deep sea dies;
The regal right
We boast to-night
Is ours through costlier sacrifice:

The blood of Vane,
His prison pain
Who traced the path the Pilgrim trod,
And hers whose faith
Drew strength from death,
And prayed her Russell up to God!

Our hearts grow cold,
We lightly hold
A right which brave men died to gain;
The stake, the cord,
The axe, the sword,
Grim nurses at its birth of pain.

The shadow rend,
And o'er us bend,
O martyrs, with your crowns and palms, —
Breathe through these throngs
Your battle songs,
Your scaffold prayers, and dungeon psalms!

Look from the sky,
Like God's great eye,
Thou solemn moon, with searching beam;
Till in the sight
Of thy pure light
Our mean self-seekings meaner seem.

  Shame from our hearts
  Unworthy arts,
The fraud designed, the purpose dark;
  And smite away
  The hands we lay
Profanely on the sacred ark.

  To party claims,
  And private aims,
Reveal that august face of Truth,
  Whereto are given
  The age of heaven,
The beauty of immortal youth.

  So shall our voice
  Of sovereign choice
Swell the deep bass of duty done,
  And strike the key
  Of time to be,
When God and man shall speak as one!

LE MARAIS DU CYGNE.

A BLUSH as of roses
  Where rose never grew!
Great drops on the bunch-grass,
  But not of the dew!
A taint in the sweet air
  For wild bees to shun!
A stain that shall never
  Bleach out in the sun!

Back, steed of the prairies!
  Sweet song-bird, fly back!
Wheel hither, bald vulture!
  Gray wolf, call thy pack!

The foul human vultures
  Have feasted and fled ;
The wolves of the Border
  Have crept from the dead.

From the hearths of their cabins,
  The fields of their corn,
Unwarned and unweaponed,
  The victims were torn, —
By the whirlwind of murder
  Swooped up and swept on
To the low, reedy fen-lands,
  The Marsh of the Swan.

With a vain plea for mercy
  No stout knee was crooked;
In the mouths of the rifles
  Right manly they looked.
How paled the May-sunshine,
  O Marais du Cygne!
On death for the strong life,
  On red grass for green!

In the homes of their rearing,
  Yet warm with their lives,
Ye wait the dead only,
  Poor children and wives!
Put out the red forge-fire,
  The smith shall not come;
Unyoke the brown oxen,
  The ploughman lies dumb.

Wind slow from the Swan's Marsh,
  O dreary death-train,
With pressed lips as bloodless
  As lips of the slain !
Kiss down the young eyelids,
  Smooth down the gray hairs;
Let tears quench the curses
  That burn through your prayers.

Strong man of the prairies,
 Mourn bitter and wild!
Wail, desolate woman!
 Weep, fatherless child!
But the grain of God springs up
 From ashes beneath,
And the crown of his harvest
 Is life out of death.

Not in vain on the dial
 The shade moves along,
To point the great contrasts
 Of right and of wrong:
Free homes and free altars,
 Free prairie and flood, —
The reeds of the Swan's Marsh,
 Whose bloom is of blood!

On the lintels of Kansas
 That blood shall not dry;
Henceforth the Bad Angel
 Shall harmless go by;
Henceforth to the sunset,
 Unchecked on her way,
Shall Liberty follow
 The march of the day.

BARBARA FRIETCHIE.

UP from the meadows rich with corn,
Clear in the cool September morn,

The clustered spires of Frederick stand
Green-walled by the hills of Maryland.

Round about them orchards sweep,
Apple- and peach-tree fruited deep,

Fair as a garden of the Lord
To the eyes of the famished rebel horde,

On that pleasant morn of the early fall
When Lee marched over the mountain-wall, —

Over the mountains winding down,
Horse and foot, into Frederick town.

Forty flags with their silver stars,
Forty flags with their crimson bars,

Flapped in the morning wind: the sun
Of noon looked down, and saw not one.

Up rose old Barbara Frietchie then,
Bowed with her fourscore years and ten;

Bravest of all in Frederick town,
She took up the flag the men hauled down;

In her attic-window the staff she set,
To show that one heart was loyal yet.

Up the street came the rebel tread,
Stonewall Jackson riding ahead.

Under his slouched hat left and right
He glanced; the old flag met his sight.

"Halt!" — the dust-brown ranks stood fast.
"Fire!" — out blazed the rifle-blast.

It shivered the window, pane and sash;
It rent the banner with seam and gash.

Quick, as it fell, from the broken staff
Dame Barbara snatched the silken scarf;

She leaned far out on the window-sill,
And shook it forth with a royal will.

"Shoot, if you must, this old gray head,
But spare your country's flag," she said.

A shade of sadness, a blush of shame,
Over the face of the leader came;

The nobler nature within him stirred
To life at that woman's deed and word:

"Who touches a hair of yon gray head
Dies like a dog! March on!" he said.

All day long through Frederick street
Sounded the tread of marching feet:

All day long that free flag tost
Over the heads of the rebel host.

Ever its torn folds rose and fell
On the loyal winds that loved it well;

And through the hill-gaps sunset light
Shone over it with a warm good-night.

Barbara Frietchie's work is o'er,
And the Rebel rides on his raids no more.

Honor to her! and let a tear
Fall, for her sake, on Stonewall's bier.

Over Barbara Frietchie's grave,
Flag of Freedom and Union, wave!

Peace and order and beauty draw
Round thy symbol of light and law;

And ever the stars above look down
On thy stars below in Frederick town!

LAUS DEO.

ON HEARING THE BELLS RING FOR THE CONSTITUTIONAL AMENDMENT ABOLISHING SLAVERY IN THE UNITED STATES.

    IT is done!
      Clang of bell and roar of gun
Send the tidings up and down.
    How the belfries rock and reel,
    How the great guns, peal on peal,
Fling the joy from town to town!

    Ring, O bells!
Every stroke exulting tells
Of the burial hour of crime.
    Loud and long, that all may hear,
    Ring for every listening ear
Of Eternity and Time!

    Let us kneel:
God's own voice is in that peal,
And this spot is holy ground.
    Lord, forgive us! What are we,
    That our eyes this glory see,
That our ears have heard the sound!

    For the Lord
On the whirlwind is abroad;
In the earthquake he has spoken;
    He has smitten with his thunder
    The iron walls asunder,
And the gates of brass are broken!

    Loud and long
Lift the old exulting song,
Sing with Miriam by the sea:
    He has cast the mighty down;
    Horse and rider sink and drown;
He has triumphed gloriously!

Did we dare,
In our agony of prayer,
Ask for more than he has done?
When was ever his right hand
Over any time or land
Stretched as now beneath the sun!

How they pale,
Ancient myth, and song, and tale,
In this wonder of our days,
When the cruel rod of war
Blossoms white with righteous law,
And the wrath of man is praise.

Blotted out!
All within and all about
Shall a fresher life begin;
Freer breathe the universe
As it rolls its heavy curse
On the dead and buried sin.

It is done!
In the circuit of the sun
Shall the sound thereof go forth.
It shall bid the sad rejoice,
It shall give the dumb a voice,
It shall belt with joy the earth!

Ring and swing
Bells of joy! on morning's wing
Send the song of praise abroad;
With a sound of broken chains,
Tell the nations that He reigns,
Who alone is Lord and God!

Cambridge: Electrotyped and Printed by Welch, Bigelow, & Co.

www.ingramcontent.com/pod-product-compliance
Lightning Source LLC
Chambersburg PA
CBHW020154170426
43199CB00010B/1034